BEATING THE SYSTEM

My Life in Foster Care

by

MARQUIS WILLIAMS

Grivante Press

ISBN-13: 978-1626768628

ISBN-10: 1626768625

BeatingTheSystem25@gmail.com

TABLE OF CONTENTS

PREFACE 5

CHAPTER 1 7

CHAPTER 2 19

CHAPTER 3 32

CHAPTER 4 43

CHAPTER 5 55

CHAPTER 6 67

CHAPTER 7 79

CHAPTER 8 89

CHAPTER 9 97

"Obstacles don't have to stop you. If you run into a wall, don't turn around and give up. Figure out how to climb it, go through it, or work around it."

- Michael Jordan

PREFACE

I contemplated writing this book for quite a long time. I've never really had a strong interest in writing prior to this endeavor, however it has been a solid skillset of mine that I have come to develop over time. My decision to write this memoir transpired after graduating from college in 2014 when I began the process of reflecting on my past and subsequently the obstacles I had overcome to reach that momentous milestone. During this process I revisited memories and experiences from my childhood that I mentally blocked out and had erased for years because I thought they were behind me. Naturally, I am an extremely private person and will typically shy away from sharing detailed personal stories about myself, even with those who are closest to me. Post graduation my work involved mentoring and advocating on behalf of youth. This work taught me the importance of being reflective, open and authentic about my past, not ashamed of it, and using my story as a means to help motivate others and bring change and awareness to common issues foster youth face. I figured there was a prime opportunity for me to publish something in this space. I hope that my story will inspire current foster youth to believe in resilience and optimism; motivate current parents and caretakers regardless of title—Biological, Foster, Legal Guardian, Adoptive etc—to provide additional encouragement, love and support; and embolden all advocators, social workers and any other professional who works directly with our most vulnerable youth population to continue to help fight for more success stories and less tragic ones.

CHAPTER 1

———

"Your problems never cease. They just change."

-Phil Jackson

I 've always been drawn to basketball. I think the first time it really became important to me was when I was about seven years old. It was recess, and I was bouncing the big orange ball. I remember the sound of other boys running around me, clumsily reaching their long, scrawny arms through crevices and cracks as I did my best to run towards the hoop. I remember the first time I made a basket- especially the way the chain crashed against the rim. It sounded like hundreds of diamonds sprinkled over the pavement. Reflecting the warmth of a Compton sun, the asphalt glimmered with hope and rejuvenation, and I knew I'd discovered my favorite pastime.

People often say that I am soft-spoken and reserved. The truth is that it is very hard for me to get close to or open up to others. There is not enough spoken direction; I'm never exactly sure what they want me to say, or where the conversation needs to go. With basketball, it's different. I know exactly what is expected of me and what I mean to the team. We communicate through our bodies, our minds and our souls. There is an underlying clairvoyance to our movements like a starling system in the sky. We ebb and flow with sacred instincts, moving towards the same goal, a spherical object falling through a hole.

I believe, similar to the realm of psychology, that we are products of both nature and nurture. My nature has always been gentle and kind, but through nurture, or the lack thereof, I've had to integrate what it means to be unwanted and unloved. When playing basketball my nature tells me where to run and jump, but when it comes to playing the game of life, there are feelings and experiences I'm not sure I'll ever understand. From the age of eight to thirteen I was a child of the foster care system. I lived in ten different homes and went to fifteen different schools. Time and time again, it became apparent to me that I was not a real part of each family, and that I would never truly belong.

We are social-creatures who long for connection and to feel as though we are a part of something. We live in a world where families are broken and ripped apart every day. The ability to find oneself through interdependent situations is becoming less and less possible all the time. We live in an individualized culture and there are many benefits to this. However, we seem to have forgotten the value of what it means to stick together like a team. It is especially difficult for a child to understand what is happening to them when they are thrown into the system. In many cases they are separated from siblings and placed in strange and unfamiliar surroundings. Social workers do their best to offer comfort and support, but in California most are overwhelmed and worn out from excessive caseloads. In this country a child enters the foster care system every two minutes. Being that there are so many of us, it's ironic that so many of us grow up feeling alone.

Like many, I never knew my father. I grew up with my Grandmother Cleo while my mother was in and out of rehab or jail for drug and theft charges. I had four older siblings who had a different father than me, and a little brother with a different father as well. Out of the three men, my father was the only one whose identity was unknown. In some ways I think this made me feel different than anyone I'd ever known. Father's Day arrived in the form of a giant question mark every year as a child. I remember watching mothers and fathers picking up the other children after school, wondering what it would be like to have parents of my own. My grandmother was great, but I still felt that I was sitting in a glass box alone while the other children lived colorful, exciting lives within family units I'd never experience.

As a young kid I recall being happy and playful enough. I received nurture and care from my grandmother and siblings and did what most little kids do. The only confusion occurred when my biological mother, Sherry, came to visit. Before I really even knew who she was, Sherry asked that we call her by her first name instead of "mom." Here was a mid-height African-American woman with a gold tooth on her upper front teeth and black hair extensions. She had a Black Panther tattoo on her neck and a Winnie the Pooh tattoo on her ankle. I never knew which way the wind was going to blow when peering into her dark brown eyes. Sherry suffered from extreme mood swings and was happy one day and sad or angry the next. I rarely saw her before the age of seven or eight. She was an alcoholic as well as a user of crack-cocaine.

In 1998 I went into the first grade and met Kate, my teacher. Kate was Caucasian, mid-height with short brown hair and brown eyes. This woman had big dreams of teaching in low socioeconomic conditions, even though she'd never personally experienced them. Starry-eyed and filled with optimism she was very upbeat, but for some reason something about her initially rubbed me the wrong way. The Teach For America program placed her in an elementary school I'd nearly been rejected from because of a long wait list. This was common at the time within Compton elementary schools, however my grandmother was very insistent that I get in, so insistent that she made a fuss with school leaders and Kate came to her side to get the administration to acquiesce. If it weren't for Kate, I might not have been in a decent school.

At first I felt resistant to this enthusiastic and happy teacher who was on a mission to help change the world. Even at the age of six I could sense her passion, and, although my brain was developing and I was still absorbing my own reality, I knew I'd seen more heartbreak than she had her in life. Kate had come from a typical white-picket-fence upbringing and sailed through college and the workforce. By the end of the school year I had become her favored. Such transparency and dedication became a bit contagious and I had nothing but respect and adoration once I realized she was real. Kate became my first solid introduction to what it is to aspire towards something positive and wholesome. Her influence would continue to inspire me for years to come.

When I was eight many things in my life began to change. Ever since I was a baby, my Grandma Cleo had taken all the children in the house to a Baptist church. For years I'd been involved in weekly Sunday school lessons, choir, and prayers. Cleo was my mother's mother and they were quite different from each other. Cleo stood four feet, ten inches tall with hazel eyes and reading glasses. She had gray, curly hair and was typically referred to as a harmless instigator

- even a meddler. If she saw something that she imagined to be disapproving in the eyes of the Almighty Lord, she'd call you out on it. Cleo was extremely religious and a bit of a do-gooder, always praising Jesus Christ and all his glory.

One day I came home from school to find my grandmother in extreme pain. She had a tremendous ache in her leg and was praying that it would go away. It wasn't working so she asked me to pray over her leg. I sat down next to her on the bed, placed my hands on her leg, and said a little prayer. Within a few days the pain went away. My grandmother saw this as a miracle and began spreading the word to her daily 5 AM prayer group that I was some kind of healer. From this point on I was asked by random people to put my hands on them and pray to bring healing. The ministers said that I was special, but I didn't really believe them. I just went along with it to appease because I was just a kid. It was definitely a weird experience, to have adults see me as something so powerful, especially since this occurred before the true difficulties of my life began.

My grandmother seemed to favor me even beyond her belief in my magical powers. I think this was because she knew she was all I had and also maybe because I didn't get in as much trouble as the other kids. My brothers and sisters were jealous of how she was with me, as she was much harsher with them. I didn't ask to be singled out, I just was. However, financial and family issues were escalating and I wouldn't be idolized for long.

In the year 2000, I entered the third grade. My grandmother was on food stamps and worked part-time as a teacher's assistant at an elementary school. Even though she couldn't read, she helped the children with coloring and artistic projects. It was around this time that Sherry started showing up at the first of each month. Sherry knew that Cleo received her food stamps in the mail at this time and strategically appeared. The money came as a paper voucher back then, so Sherry would take it and run. Then she'd sell it for cash so she could buy alcohol or drugs.

Over time the confrontation between daughter and mother was getting more and more violent. I remember one time hearing Sherry ask for the money and my grandmother said, "No."

"If you don't give me the money," Sherry said, "I'm going to tear this place apart."

My grandmother tried to hold her ground but Sherry was coming down off of crack and started throwing things in the house. Somehow Cleo threw Sherry out of the house, but just when I thought she'd gone I heard a loud crash. I went out to the living room to find a hole in our front window through which Sherry had thrown a giant rock! I was irate.

This behavior continued and soon Sherry was using us to threaten Cleo. She'd say, "I'm going to take my children and put them in a foster home. You know I'll do it. I've done it before."

It was true. About five years earlier one of the oldest siblings had voluntarily gone into the foster care system due to Sherry's encouragement. This had put our family onto the Department of Children and Family Services radar and a case was opened. Sherry had been hysterical many times while screaming at Cleo for messing everything up by taking her children. She blamed and accused her of stealing us children. As a teenager, Sherry was very rebellious and ran away from home often. My grandfather remarried and left when Sherry was young. He always valued his new family more than he valued Cleo or Sherry. This was very hard for both of them.

After months of fighting, my grandmother had enough and called The Department of Children & Family Services. Cleo was our legal guardian and Sherry's threats really had no weight, but Cleo felt it was the best way of protecting us. My grandmother did her best to explain this to my little brother, Danger, and myself. She sat us down and said, "I know this is going to be hard to understand, but I've run out of options. I'm stressed and fed up with Sherry. I don't know exactly what is going to happen, but I want you both to be prepared." I didn't really think much of it at the time.

Three days later my mother found out that Cleo was planning on actually putting us in the foster care system. Even though she'd said this was what she wanted, Sherry went crazy and came after us. Technically she kidnapped Danger and me, along with an older sibling who was no longer a minor. We slept in her 1970 white Cadillac for a few days and ate McDonald's. Even though it was summertime, I remember feeling cold under a thin blanket during those nights.

I felt very torn during this time. Danger was only four-years old and I felt protective of him, but Sherry was making promises to us about how things were going to change and that she was going to take care of us. I was excited about my mother getting better, but I felt like I was betraying my grandmother. Sherry believed she was protecting us from Cleo and the foster care system. Extended family had gotten involved and everyone was pushing for Sherry to meet with a social worker. I don't know if it was because of her addictions or the realization that she was not prepared to truly be a mother, but she gave in and drove us to the address she'd been given over the phone.

The Cadillac's brakes weren't working well and Sherry was drinking and driving. We were running late as we drove towards the relative's house that had set everything up. We crashed into the gate when we got there. I remember Sherry signing some papers and then saying goodbye to us. She promised she'd do whatever she could to get clean, get a job, and have a place for us to live. I was horrified and didn't understand what was happening. From there the social worker took Danger and me to her car and drove us straight to the first foster care family's house.

First grade class photo in 1998, I'm second front row (L-R)

Me, my grandmother and Danger at the end of my first grade school in year 1999 (L-R)

CHAPTER 2

———

"There can only be one state of mind as you approach any profound test; total concentration, a spirit of togetherness, and strength."

-Pat Riley

Danger and I cried as the social worker drove us the eleven miles from Compton to Long Beach. We really had no idea what was happening. My heart hurt terribly and my hands were sweating. I put my arms around Danger and held him close as I watched palm trees and SUV's whiz past us. The California sun beat through the backseat window and onto my leg. I could feel it heating up the top of my thigh, and for a second I felt a vague sense of relaxation—but then it quickly passed.

We arrived at Marla and Jim's three-bedroom home quicker than I expected. This was a retired African-American couple, only we hardly saw Jim, and spent most of our time with Marla. Marla was a big-boned intimidating woman, although when we first met her we thought she was sweet. That night I was so terrified at what was happening I accidentally wet the bed.

Marla screamed and yelled at me the next morning, "You are too old for this, ya hear me? Whatcha want? Me to buy you diapers? You not no baby! Thank God this is only temporary!"

Like acclimating a dog or a cat to a new place, for the first couple of days Danger and I stayed inside watching TV. Marla was like a parrot, repeating over and over that this was just temporary and that if we behaved we'd be placed in a more permanent home. Danger adjusted okay after a day or two. He stopped crying for my grandmother and nestled up next to me. For me it was different. I didn't have anyone else to look up to. I was spiraling out into the vastness of a cosmic void with no gravity, planets or stars to pull me. I was floating aimlessly. I didn't know what to think, so I let my mind drift away with the cartoons and sitcoms on the screen.

On the third day we ventured into the backyard to play. Behind the lawn there was an alley and a shed off to the right of it. Danger and I were roleplaying as if we were Power Rangers, superheroes doing our best to outsmart the evil Ivan Ooze. While outside that day, we suddenly heard a crash. Someone was breaking into the back shed. Marla's big eyes appeared at the window, wide as ever as she spotted the intruder. She ushered us into the house, called the police, and we sat on the couch waiting. The guy ran off by the time the cops got there, but it was still traumatizing. We had just started to let loose a little when a threat reappeared. It was added fuel to an already chaotic fire.

On the fourth day we had our first court appearance. I was dressed in my Sunday best and felt myself sweating through the suit as we arrived at the courthouse. I'd never been in a courtroom before. I'd only seen savvy defense attorneys or no-nonsense prosecutors stirring up the jury on shows like *Law & Order* or *NYPD Blues*. The social worker led Danger and me down a long hall and into a private room where Cleo was waiting for us. It had been nearly two weeks since I'd seen her.

My grandmother jumped up from her chair and ran over to us. She could tell by the look on my face that I was not pleased. Danger hugged her and then she asked me, "Marquis, can I get a hug?"

I felt rage burning in my chest. How could she do this to us? What was she thinking? Did she really think Marla was a better fit than she was? How could any of this be better for us? "No," I said it point-blank and with disdain. "No," I repeated again, in case she hadn't heard me. As I turned to walk out of the room I could hear her crying.

From a glance I saw Sherry and my siblings during the court session. Danger and I officially became wards of the state, and then the judge checked in with everyone to review arrangements and to figure out what was best for the family. My grandmother had her own lawyer, as did Sherry. Danger and I had a lawyer too. Every six months, these court appearances occurred. In the system, a social worker's job is to stay connected to a foster kid, take notes, and then present his or her update to the court where the case would be reviewed. There was no jury, only a judge who has the final say.

During that first session, Cleo waived her legal rights; so from that point on she sat and observed the proceedings, but did not participate. In the early days Sherry had convinced herself that she would be able to get her life together so that we could live with her. In order for this to happen she'd have to get clean by going to rehab, get a job, and rent an apartment. This would have to be the case for at least six months before custody would be considered. It was Sherry's lawyer's job to prove she could do these things. The effort was short-lived, however. Over time Sherry's enthusiasm dwindled.

During that first court appearance, I made it clear that I did not want to live with anyone but my grandmother, even though I was furious with her. The judge said that visits might be an option but not at that time. I'd told my lawyer that I did not like Marla, so he told my social worker and she arranged for another move.

Taken after our first of many court appearances
(2001)

There are two types of social workers that I came across throughout the years. The first type were the ones who truly believed in their work and felt empathy and compassion for the children they served. These were the ones who really listened to what I said to them, and did their best to make things better. The second type were those who lacked sympathy and were just doing

24

their jobs and going through the motions. They didn't listen and instead made decisions based on what they thought was best without considering the child's feelings. Over the years I had four social workers, all of whom were women. The social worker that worked with me in the beginning was very nice, which to this day I am grateful for.

If I'd known that Danger and I would be divided, I might have pushed staying with Marla instead. I didn't know though, I didn't understand most of what was happening to me. One week after my court hearing the social worker drove us to the next home in Carson, California. Once out of the car she told me that I would be living here, but that a different social worker would be taking my brother to another home. My knees buckled and I felt as though I'd been punched hard in the stomach. Tears streamed from my eyes as I ran to Danger. I was sobbing, so he sobbed too. I hugged him hard and screamed when the other social worker arrived, and the two women tried to pull us apart. What were they doing? How could they do this to a four-year-old kid? He needed me. I needed him. He was all I had left.

The other social worker picked up Danger, placed him in her car and drove off. I remember the look on Danger's face: it was frantic, heartbroken and filled with fear. He was like a helpless otter pup, being dragged away from his mother by an alligator. I could see his mouth through the glass, calling out my name. The vision burned into my brain and sat with me for years.

The second family I lived with was in a small, single-parent home run by a twenty-six-year-old woman named Jesse. She had a seven-year-old son, Willis. They were African-American as well- nine of the ten families I lived with were. Jesse was pretty tough; she spoke loud and obnoxiously. She was also very aggressive even though she was a tiny, little person. She liked to argue with people on the phone or with whoever stopped by to visit. I think she might have had a drinking problem, because she drank directly from the liquor bottle on a nightly basis after work.

Jesse was nice to me, but I noticed that she took her anger out on Willis often. This bothered me, but there was nothing I could do about it. I liked Willis. We spent most of our time playing video games. While Jesse was at work, her mother watched us boys during the day. It was still summertime of 2000, so I put my mind into the *PlayStation* video game while eating popsicles and candy. During that month with Jesse and Willis, I began to feel myself start to melt away. When a glacier of pain sits waiting to be chiseled into something magnificent or supreme, but you don't have the strength, it's easier just to hope it'll melt. After a few weeks of crying myself to sleep, I successfully pushed that glacier out of my mind and let the world's distractions convince me I'd be okay.

A new situation was forming while I drowned out my days with video games. My grandmother's niece had become a foster parent and was open to taking me in. The arrangement would be that Danger would join us a month later. I decided to do it. School was going to start soon, so I would begin the fourth grade in a new school while living with my first cousin once removed. Her name was Margaret and she was around thirty-five years old. She was single and already had two other foster kids. Margaret looked similar to Sherry but her energy was positive. But also, she had a preconceived notion about Danger and me. Apparently we'd already been deemed "bad kids" through the familial grapevine.

The other foster kids were named Jack, aged eight, and Bobbie, aged thirteen. They were automatically considered "good kids" to Margaret and she definitely treated them differently. They'd been living with her for over three years already, and they acted like a tight-knit family. Danger was still too little to notice, but I felt out of place. Margaret also held a strong Christian faith and so again I found myself back at our old Baptist church. There I was able to see my grandmother once a week.

Over time, my love for my grandmother superseded my anger. When you're taken from those you love and placed in a strange new environment, harsh feelings fade away. Like a shell or armor, over time the hardness dissolved and I found myself back inside the heart. While I still didn't completely understand Cleo's actions, I knew I would never stop loving her and would always want to be with her the most. She was after all, my first introduction to a mother.

Seeing her at church was bittersweet. It was a relief to talk to her, see her face and feel her affections. Then when it was time to leave, it was like my heart broke all over again and I became stuffed with anger and confusion. I lived with Margaret for nearly four months and every single week my heart shattered into a thousand pieces. It was like I was strapped into the Riddler's Revenge ride at Six Flags Magic Mountain—only it wasn't exhilarating, it was awful. I was thrown up and down and all around, over and over and over.

I lived in Bellflower, California at this point, in a nice part of town. The school was cleaner and nicer than those I'd been to before. It was obvious that the materials, the building, and even the staff were good quality. While it was nice to be back in school as a way of spreading out my time with Margaret and a family I didn't feel a part of, I had a hard time getting along with other children and didn't really have any friends. The roller coaster of emotions I was experiencing was too distracting to settle into the normal, productive routines of each day. I felt defiant towards authority and already had it in my head that no one would really want to be friends with me.

Why would I have trusted any authority figures at that point? They'd betrayed the most basic trust a child has: they'd stripped me of all sense of security. Like a stray, I'd been thrown into the back of a dogcatcher's truck and taken to a shelter. I'd been placed inside a cage, and occasionally through the bars, someone would pet me, but no one really wanted to take me. Most people were only interested in the puppies or kittens because there was something instinctively maternal about bringing an animal up from a young age. It made more sense. What if the stray dog had been abused or suffered from some unknown ailment that might just make it snap one day? Could anyone really trust a stray like me?

I wasn't going to allow myself to open up; it was too risky. So I began to become what I'd already been deemed: a troublemaker. My school was throwing its annual PTA school fundraiser, and whatever class brought in the most money would get a pizza party. My teacher was pretty certain we were going to win, which meant we had the most money. I talked to Margaret's other foster son, Jack about it. We made a plan to steal the money. Jack and Bobbie were a little like Batman's Two-Face character, they were sweet as cherubs around Margaret, but behind her back they became little villains. Not to say that I was a saint by any means, I just didn't put on the good front. During lunch, I lunged into the classroom and towards my teacher's desk. With hands shaking and heart racing, I rummaged around until I found the money in an orange envelope. I folded it, put it in my pocket and ran out of the room as quickly as I could.

CHAPTER 3

———

"I often tell people when you make a mistake, you not only hurt yourself, but you hurt the ones you love."

-Magic Johnson

L ater that day my teacher saw the giant bulge in my pocket and walked over to me in a rage. She took my arm and led me straight to the principal's office. I was in big, big trouble. Margaret was called and came to pick me up from school. She was furious and screamed at me once I was in the car. I sat in the backseat as we drove through the streets with my head in my hands. Once we came to a stop sign Margaret turned around, still in a fury, and threw a shoe from the front seat at my head.

"What the hell is the matter with you boy? Do you think stealing is going to get you anywhere in life? Are you stupid? You think anyone's going to want to take you in now? You think anyone is going to care about a little dumb ass like you? No one wants a thief in their home, especially me!"

At that point, I opened the door and jumped out of the car. I ran through a nice, upscale neighborhood past perfectly cut lawns and spic and span windows and cars. Eventually I came to a man sitting on his front porch. I was out of breath but asked with panic oozing from my voice, "Hey, can you tell me where I am?" I wasn't sure what I was going to do, but I knew I wanted to find a payphone to call my grandmother.

Before he had a chance to respond Margaret's teal blue Hyundai Excel pulled up in front of me. "Get in this car boy! Right now!" She put the car in park and acted like she was going to run after me. I knew I had to go with her; there was no other way.

The man on the porch looked relieved as we drove off. Inside the car Margaret seemed extremely overwhelmed and emotional, and I felt bad for her. "You could have been kidnapped," she said through mixed emotions. She was still angry, but I think more than anything, she was truly terrified. She really had no idea what to do with me.

A few weeks later, Margaret told us that Danger and I would be sent to a new home. She told the social workers that it was because she needed to move into a smaller home, and that she would no longer be able to care for Jack or Bobbie either. I never ratted out Jack and took the fall for him instead. He never stepped up to share the blame but pretended to be shocked at my behavior. Danger hadn't done anything wrong, but Margaret felt he should go too. I was worried that Danger and I would be split up again, and devastated that even family couldn't handle taking us in.

The same awful scenario played itself out as Danger and I were ripped apart a second time. We cried and screamed while doing our best to stay attached: little hands latching onto littler hands. There was nothing we could do, we were pulled away from each other and taken to different cities.

The fourth family I lived with was located in Compton, an older couple in their sixties. The man wasn't around very much but the woman, Nadine was, and was nice and warm in the beginning. I was terribly upset about Danger and didn't receive a word about him for three or four months after I got there. I remember feeling melancholy and glum, like I could have protected him. I thought about how I'd jumped out of Margaret's car and ran away. I wondered if I had what it would take to live on the streets supporting Danger and myself. I thought of different escape routes and master plans to find Danger and to leave, but in the end I was always too afraid.

After a while I heard from Cleo that Margaret had not moved into a smaller house and had not given Jack or Bobbie back to the state. I understand now how difficult it would be to take on four boys as a single foster parent and do not blame her for lessening the load. She was a genuinely good person and probably felt obligated or pressured by family members to look after us. Later on, Margaret apologized for giving us up and told me that she was sorry it didn't work out.

After staying with Nadine for a while, I eventually heard from a social worker that Danger was doing well. This eased my stress a little and I tried to put my head into the fifth grade. However, it was hard to concentrate and to learn new things. I was falling behind, but had started to play basketball at recess, which brought a sense of contentment.

Nadine was loving and kind, and after about six months, the idea of adoption came up. I felt awkward and skittish about it. At this point I'd been assigned to a new social worker. This woman was only twenty-one and much less sensitive and in-tune than the previous one. She was constantly clashing with and behaving combatively towards others including Sherry. During a meeting, she said to me, "Marquis, it doesn't look like your mom is going to be able to get herself together enough to get you back. Since you like Nadine and Robert, how would you feel about making it permanent? Adoption?"

I didn't know how to respond. I was afraid if I said no they'd move me to a different home, but at the same time I wasn't sure if I wanted to be adopted by someone I didn't know that well. A few weeks later everything changed, so I didn't have to make the decision. Nadine's grandchildren came to live with her and she transformed into something less sweet and more—'threatened.' (I suppose that is the perfect word). There were three grandkids: a fifteen-year-old girl, and two boys, aged six and ten. Somehow the presence of her own kin put Nadine on the defensive. It was as if the cubs had returned to Grandma Bear and I was the odd wolf pup suddenly realizing I would never be part of the family.

Luckily I'd started to see my own grandmother on the weekends. She was allowed to visit me for a few hours every Saturday. I felt at this point that I'd fully forgiven Cleo and understood that she'd put us in the system because she believed it was to protect us. More than anything, I just missed being around her and people who truly knew me. We had so much fun on those Saturday outings. We'd go get ice cream, go to the movies, the park or the zoo. I always returned feeling elated at our time together, but also sad that I couldn't be with her every day.

Nadine's grandkids were very jealous of Cleo and me and the enjoyment we had together. They saw our special bond, and resented it. They were mad that they couldn't go with Cleo and me to see movies or to buy candy too. In response, the grandkids made me feel like I should choose them over her. I think this behavior was because they were never taken anywhere, and in a way I felt bad about that, but there was nothing I could do about it. I'm sure those children were coping with issues with their own parents—in essence, we were all struggling to find comfort and security, wherever we could.

I was miserable and wished I could just go live with my grandmother again, but the problem was that she didn't have her own place anymore and was living with her sister. It just didn't seem possible. The social workers and Nadine agreed that adoption wasn't a good idea, which was a relief. Still, a fiery ball of rage was growing inside of my stomach, heart and chest. Nothing seemed fair and no one would take me under his or her wing to make me feel like things were going to be okay. Nadine and her grandchildren were ostracizing me more and more each day. I still didn't have friends at school, and I hadn't seen my brother for months. Inevitably, I started having real problems at school.

I was defiant and rebellious towards all authority figures. I would purposely not follow directions, be painfully disruptive and not pay attention. I'd build walls out of my pencils, daydream, and constantly tap my feet or hands on the desk to infuriate my teachers. I was no longer the sweet little boy Cleo had deemed a miracle worker. Now I was a pissed-off kid with nothing to lose. If I'd had a superhero costume that best depicted my emblem at the time, it would have been made of two words: SCREW YOU. I was suspended and sent to different schools four times that year. After a while my behavior took its toll on Nadine, and she told the social worker to start looking for another place for me to live.

Just before moving out of Nadine's house, I received a phone call from Kate, my first grade teacher. Before Cleo gave us to the state I'd become quite close to Kate. I saw her up until the third grade where she would give me rides to school, and take a few other students and me on outings. Kate eventually found out what happened to me and like a dove soaring through a cloudy sky, she brought a message of peace.

She told me she was leaving town for graduate school in Massachusetts but that she wanted to keep in touch. We began to exchange letters, origami, cards, and fun little games and puzzles. Her reaching out was like a breath of fresh air that helped me rise above the whirlpool I kept getting sucked into. She gave me faith that someone was thinking about me, looking out for me and genuinely cared about my wellbeing. In order for Kate to visit me she had to request permission from a judge and wait to be cleared. It took months for this to happen.

Every time I was sent to a new family, it was court-ordered that within the first thirty days of being there, I received a psychological and medical evaluation. The new care providers would have access to old files and my history, and the new foster parents would receive a big black binder with all of my previous experiences documented within. This big black book was passed around and added to on my account for years. The foster parent could read every single detail about my past, my grades and my medical records. I felt chained to that book, as if it were shackled to my leg and that everywhere I went it went too. I was a prisoner to my past and with each new family I was squeezed into the tiny holes of a pillory, naked, vulnerable and exposed to public shame.

The fifth family that I lived with only lived one block away from Nadine. The house was tidy and well kept. The family consisted of a working couple in their fifties, a son who'd already moved out, and a sixteen-year-old son who still lived there. The father, Calvin, worked a lot and the mother, June, was very straightforward and militant in her discipline. Timing and structure were the foundations of that household. We were to eat at specific times and by god, we'd better eat everything on our plates. We were to make our beds immaculately every morning, keep the house spotless, and abide by specific regimens and chores. June even made sure her son and I both peed sitting down instead of standing up.

The second day after I arrived June took me to see a psychiatrist for my psychological evaluation. Unlike the other foster parents, June sat in the room with me. The shrink asked me questions about diet, eating habits, sleep, concentration and my attention span. He asked, "Marquis, do you find yourself daydreaming a lot?"

Immediately June replied, "Yes, he does."

I am not nor have I ever been what one would call a fast communicator. I take my time thinking about things and formulating sentences before speaking. I had no time to respond to the doctor throughout most of the session because June kept doing it for me. By the time the hour was up, I'd been diagnosed ADHD and prescribed Ritalin. I'm not sure what June's intentions were, even now in retrospect, and why she was pushing medication. However, in the foster care system foster, parents who take in a child with special needs, or mental or physical disabilities in the state of California typically receive additional monthly benefits for taking in the child. Maybe June genuinely thought I would be better off on the meds, or maybe she wanted to milk every last dime out of me that she could.

CHAPTER 4

"Everything happens for a reason. I'm used to it, I prepare for it. Like I say, at the end of the day, those in charge of their own destiny are going to do what's right for them and their family."

-Shaquille O'Neal

I was not at June and Calvin's home for long-maybe two or three weeks. The Ritalin made me feel wired, and messed with my moods and emotions. I would secretly not take it when no one was looking, or I'd spit it out later if June eyed me while I "washed it down" with a glass of water. The ups and downs from the stimulant were agonizing, to say the least. I didn't realize it at the time, but the roller coaster ride of Ritalin most likely echoed the ups and downs that

Sherry experienced to a degree. How strange that even when we have no control over something, the patterns of our lineage creep in when no one is paying attention.

With my moods more erratic than ever, I was suspended from school again. I was sent home and ordered to sit on June's impeccably clean green couch for the reckoning. Both Calvin and June were angry and the energy of the room filled with suspense. There was a threatening undertone that made me shift uncomfortably as they drilled the importance of doing well in school into my head.

"Do you even realize that you're playing with fire, boy?" Calvin's graying hairline moved in accordance with his furrowed forehead, accentuating his distress. He reminded me of Mo from *The Simpsons,* only he was black and getting redder and redder by the minute.

"Yeah," June chimed in, "you want to end up some stupid idiot who can't make a dime because you never learned anything worthwhile? Don't be a damn fool! We took you in, we are giving you everything, and you are acting like an ungrateful boy!"

My palms were sweating and I could feel my heart begin to race. Calvin's demeanor was growing larger and more intimidating like a mean dog's shadow made large from the light of a fire cast onto a cave wall. I thought maybe I should get up and run. Something unfavorable was brewing inside that man's head. He began yelling about how ungrateful I was, unhitched his belt buckle, and slid it out from the loops on his pants.   Carefully, he folded the belt perfectly equal, pulling it taut, then releasing it and pulling it tight with a loud warning "crack!"   He was letting me know he wasn't messing around. That was it. I'd seen enough. I wasn't going to stick around to get beat by someone I barely knew. In a flash, I ran to the front door and out of the house.

My feet flew across the cracks and divots on the sidewalk as I made my way back to the school. I knew at least there, some authority figure would know what to do. I ran to the front desk and told the secretary that I needed to contact my social worker immediately. The school counselor located my file and helped me make the call. A half an hour later, the social worker called back to let me know I could stay at Nadine's until she figured out where to take me next.

The next morning the social worker came and picked me up. We didn't go back to June's to get my things, so I lost all of my belongings. I had pictures, toys, and a few articles of clothes that were lost forever. I was bummed about my stuff, but at the same time I was relieved I wouldn't have to see their angry faces again. I was off to someplace new.

From Compton to Long Beach I went, which was about thirty minutes away. This was a bittersweet situation because on the one hand I liked the sixth family I lived with, but on the other it was much more difficult for my grandmother to visit me. She'd have to take the bus, which would make her commute take two hours or more both ways. Since this was the case, I only saw Cleo about once a month. Things were still going well for us, we loved each other and that was the way it was going to stay.

Rhonda was a stay-at-home mom in her thirties. She had another foster care boy named Darrell who was seven. Rhonda was average-sized and had a very fun-loving temperament. She did not work, but lived off the foster money and some government assistance. We lived in a two-bedroom apartment in a great part of town. I shared a room with Darrell, who had a hamster. Lucky for me, I started at a magnet school to finish out the 5th grade in the spring of 2003. A magnet school has special courses and intense specialized curriculum, emphasis are put on diversity as well. If a magnet school is in your home district you're automatically accepted in most cases.

I stayed with Rhonda and Darrell for almost a year. I kept receiving letters and phone calls from Kate, and saw Cleo when she had time to make the commute. I had realized a lot from my earlier foster care days. I was getting older and saw how much harder things were when I resisted them. June and Calvin's intimidation tactics had completed a transformation that had been in the works for a while. I was a baby bluebird who'd been ripped out of the nest and tossed back and forth from owl, to seagull to vulture. At first I tried to defy what was happening to me, but the rebellion was only making things worse. The fact of the matter was, that where and whom I was placed with, was really out of my control. My destiny was still unknown, but my fate was currently not my own.

It was time to let myself feel okay again, and to relax with Rhonda and Darrell. I was starting to do better at school. I stopped hating authority figures as much and I realized that I actually liked a lot of my teachers. I started to make friends who also loved playing basketball at recess every single day. Rhonda and Darrell liked to play board games, so we were always engaged in some kind of fun activity.

Part of the reason that I was in a good place probably had something to do with the fact that secretly I wasn't taking the medication prescribed for my "ADHD." I was supposed to take the Ritalin every other day but I was going weeks without taking it. After a while, Rhonda started watching to make sure I took it. She just wanted to follow protocol and make sure I was doing what I was supposed to. I was about ten months into my stay with them, and at this point things changed again.

I was taking the Ritalin as prescribed and it was altering my moods significantly. I felt like I was going to snap. The constant buzz from the upper caused me to feel anxious and uneasy, and then the comedown made me feel hollow and depressed. My soul was being stretched, yanked, and pulled into different shapes and sizes like Play-Doh. I couldn't see straight, I couldn't see behind or in front of me, it was just a blur of colors caused from constant spinning. And then—I did snap.

I'd been having emotional outbursts where it felt as if the Hulk took over my body. I'd scream and yell at Rhonda about random things. Within a few weeks my rage hit its peak and I tackled Darrell. The kid had tested my last nerve. He liked to mimic whatever I said, and did things to fire me up. That last time it was like the flame that lit the dynamite, and everything blew to bits. I sat on his little frame, pinning down his arms and shoulders with my legs while punching him in the face. Rhonda came into the room and pulled me off of him before any real damage was done. I was so angry my hands were shaking.

All of that sorrow and sadness from loss and abandonment had been funneled through the medium of fury and mania. My little three-family utopia would never be the same. Once a friend, I was now seen as a threat and a loose cannon. I probably should have told someone that I didn't like the Ritalin, but psychiatrists, professionals, foster moms, and adults in general all seemed to know better about what was best for me. It was hard enough for me to speak about my emotions, let alone formulate opinions or exercise my little boy willpower in a world of giants and titans.

Rhonda hinted about how I might want to live somewhere else. At first I ignored this sentiment completely. The dangers of letting in, the implications were too great. I had come to love living there, and I felt affectionate towards Rhonda, and even Darrell. The idea that I would once again be rejected by those I loved was too much to make its way to comprehension. After a while, Rhonda's tiptoeing around the truth of her intentions eventually fell on middle ground.

"Marquis," she began, "I've spoken with your social worker and she wants you to try out living with a man, just for the weekend. He's really nice and he loves fishing. In fact, he wants to teach you how to catch a fish. Would you like that?"

I shrugged my shoulders and nodded my head from side to side. "I don't know. I guess."

"Okay, great," she said. "The social worker will pick you up tomorrow and drive you out to

Bill's house to spend the night with him. I'm sure you guys will have a lot of fun."

I looked into her eyes and saw sincerity, but I also saw commitment to conviction staring back at me. She'd already made her mind up; she preferred their life without me.

Bill was the only Caucasian I ever stayed with. He was heavy-set, in his forties and had a balding head, which he attempted to cover up with a comb-over. He lived about ten minutes away from Rhonda in a two-bedroom home. It was just the two of us. I got there in the morning on a Saturday and Bill already had his truck packed and ready for us to go fishing. We drove thirty minutes down a dirt road until we came to the location he called "his lucky spot," which was on a dock on a lake. I'd never been fishing before, so it took him about twenty minutes to explain how the rod, hook, string and reel all worked together. I liked it after I got the hang of it.

Bill was a man of few words and came across a little weird, but not in a bad way. He didn't talk about himself very much. He only said that he wanted to find someone to adopt. It seemed that he felt adoption was an ethical and virtuous endeavor, and that by taking in someone that needed a guardian he'd be paying it forward. Bill kept asking me questions about my family of origin and if I intended to live with them again. I said yes. I think at this point Bill realized that I wasn't the right fit. He was a good guy, but after attending a kid's birthday party the next day, I was taken back to Rhonda's to see where the wind would blow me next.

A week later a new social worker came to pick me up. This social worker, Jessica, was really great. She looked like she was in her late thirties, had gold dreadlocks and spoke with a Caribbean accent. She listened to me and genuinely cared. Out of all the social workers I had, she was my favorite. Jessica would call me once or twice a week and ask how I was doing, or how I was feeling. She also seemed to understand a lot of the issues I was dealing with, and that ultimately I was unhappy because I wanted to go home to my grandma. Jessica kept an open communication with Cleo to keep her in the loop. She was very aware of what was going on in my life and wanted to find the right fit for me.

"Marquis," she said, "I don't think things are working out here with Rhonda. I'm going to find a place that'll be better for you. Don't you worry, it'll all work out." Jessica winked at me, patted my back and said, "Keep your chin up, everything will be okay."

I couldn't help but feel devastated. It was like being told by someone else that's your close friend they didn't want to be friends anymore. I understood that Rhonda would have had a hard time saying that she didn't want me there, but she could have been more straightforward about her feelings. The week after staying with Bill, I thought things were going back to normal with Rhonda and Darrell. Apparently I was wrong.

I was sad about it but acted like I was fine, I made Rhonda think I was ready to go. I pretended as best a ten-year-old could that I wasn't hurt. I wouldn't give her the satisfaction. Deep down I was slowly being sucked down to the ocean floor, where darkness reigned and the water pressure from above threatened implosion. Even though internally I was being squeezed to the point of collapse, on the surface I made her think I was water skiing in the sun. I felt apathetic after a while; I mean what was the point of having the ebb and flow of relationship honesty and growth, if I was never going to see that seventh family ever again? There was no point.

In my mind it was easier to see them as a story I'd scribbled into a notebook. After a few weeks, I went back, read the story and realized it was stupid. So I burned it, and just like that, it was forever erased from existence. No one would ever have to know that it'd been written, because there was no proof, no evidence. I watched the paper fold into a black ball and then float off as ash in the wind. It was a strange feeling, driving away from Rhonda's, the dichotomy of experiencing such love, and then such rejection felt like the two cancelled each other out. So I wiped the slate clean and started over.

Each family created a new layer. Like Russian dolls, the Inner Marquis grew further and further away from what I was on the outside. I was done. I'd adopt a stoic approach to life and make sure not to give my fragility away to others anymore.

CHAPTER 5

---

*"My character has always been important to me.
That was the one thing I knew, no matter what, I had
to hold that strong."*

-Derek Fisher

T he eighth family lived in Pomona, California, forty-five minutes away from my last home. This was a large family with three other foster children: two teenage girls aged sixteen and seventeen, and another boy my age. We lived in a four-bedroom house with the mother, Jasmine, who was in her mid-forties, and her retired parents who were in their seventies. Jasmine was thin, short, and had long dark hair. She was somewhat polite but was also easily angered. She was very much a disciplinarian - a little like June had been.

I began middle school in a new district and was pretty pleased with the neighborhood and general ambiance. It was clean and quiet. I enjoyed the freedom that came along with being in middle school and was pretty content with Jasmine and the family. I took the opportunity once again to start over and try not to create waves. I was actually improving academically, driven most likely by my new willpower to succeed. Luckily after the psychological evaluation, I was told that I was not ADHD and could go off the Ritalin.

This was a do-over for me. I was sick of being thrown around. My new approach was to be a "good kid" so I could stay at one place long enough to feel grounded. Maybe Cleo would be able to take me back, maybe I could just toughen it out for another seven or eight years till I graduated or emancipate. I just wanted things to settle and gel. For about two months, that's what happened.

During this time Kate finished grad school and moved to New York City to work at the Teach For America headquarters. The organization paid for her apartment in New York and also for flights to Los Angeles every two weeks. Kate had been given special privileges in my case and was allowed visitation rights. She had an apartment in Venice Beach. This was walking distance from the iconic Venice Beach basketball courts. Twice a month we'd hang out, go to the beach and shoot hoops for hours.

Kate was able to pick up Danger and bring him with us. This really filled my heart with hope and love again. I'd missed both of them very much. It seemed that as foster kids, we mostly spent our time indoors. I don't know if this is because foster parents were worried about us being kidnapped or running away, but our activities typically included video games, television, and the occasional board game. Going out into nature, being outside with the fresh air and sun shining on our faces with Kate was amazing. Again the metaphor of being dogs and pups in a kennel played itself out. With Kate we were able to run, jump, swing, laugh, and even fly with the freedom of imagination once again taking the stage. I was beginning to feel the difference between the temporary and the permanent. Kate presented Danger and me with something solid and consistent.

Beyond getting us outside, Kate also liked to talk and ask questions. Her energy was positive, uplifting, and really very nurturing. I didn't like to talk. In fact I was growing more and more introverted and quiet, but somehow she got me to spill my feelings. Kate was very therapeutic and wanted to know if there was anything she could do to help. She often said, "I'm here for you now and I always will be.

"You guys should never be afraid to tell me anything you want and I won't judge you. I will always advocate for you. "

Danger was about six years old and was developing differently than I had. He was more adaptable; maybe due to his foster care journey starting at a more impressionable age. Many times, Kate would take us to Danger's flag football games. We'd eat pizza, drink Gatorade, and cheer when Danger scored. I think because of the joy I felt when I was with people that actually loved me, returning to Jasmine's home felt plastic, or like I was walking onto the set of a family television series. The actors and actresses read their lines with shallow sentiment. Their connections were skin-deep and came across as forced or oblique. It wasn't their fault though; it was the director and writers who were to blame. The truth was that it was just a story; it wasn't a real family. We weren't being honest about the absurdity of our charade.

I started getting into fights with the other foster boy my age, James, over whose turn it was to play video games. James and I would yell and hit each other over Xbox feuds. James would run and tell Jasmine that I hit him, so then everyone else in the family would blame me. I was becoming the black sheep once again.

"What the hell is wrong with you, Marquis?" Jasmine had asked with fury wavering in her voice. "Why can't you share? Are you just a little, selfish shit who was never taught to be a decent kid? You think because you're here that you can just do whatever you want? Hit James and get away with it? I don't think so!" She screamed. "You got another thing coming if you continue this!"

Maybe it was the strength I'd been given through Kate, and a secure feeling that she'd always have my back. Maybe it was the stoic temperament that had kept me emotionally distant and safe from giving too much to others. Whatever it was, I could no longer hold back, and

I let her have it. "SHUT THE F*** UP!" I yelled at the top of my lungs, and then darted out the front door, leaving her in shock.

I had a flashback of June and Calvin, especially of Calvin with that belt clenched tight between his fists. I wasn't going to put up with another adult threatening to hurt me or put me down. I hadn't given much to Jasmine, James, or the others in the family. I'd done this on purpose, to keep myself distant and detached. Still, they could take something I wasn't giving from me, they could call me names, make me the bad guy, or worse: they could hit me and leave bruises and welts. My biological mother had struck me a few times when she was raging and coming down off of crack. I must have developed an internal compass for navigating the potential for violence, because I was out of Jasmine's house before she could start counting to three.

I tried to call my social worker at a gas station but couldn't reach her. Just as I left the store a cop whirled next to me. He asked what was my name then said to get in the front seat of the car. He explained my guardian had called because I ran away. I was solemn and quiet as we drove through the neighborhood in the afternoon heat.

"What's the matter kid?" The cop asked.

"I don't want to go back there," I muttered.

"What was that?" he asked.

"I don't want to go back there," I said again with more volume and angst.

"You just hold tight," he said as we pulled up in front of the house. "I'll go talk to your foster mom and I'll be right back."

I watched from the window as the police officer rapped on the door and exchanged a few words with Jasmine. She looked angry and pointed at the car while verbalizing biting words I could only imagine were laced with venom.

The officer walked back to his car, opened the door and climbed inside. The leather seat made a funny noise as he got settled, but I didn't laugh or giggle. "Well," he began, "looks like you two have reached an agreement. She doesn't want you there either. Guess we're heading to the station. I'm Officer Sanchez. What's your story Mr. Marquis?"

I felt relieved and chatted as much as I could with the funny, warm-hearted cop. I sat at the police station for nearly eight hours. The cops told me they were waiting to hear back from my social worker. It was the weekend, so things were moving slowly. The police officers said Jessica was looking for an emergency placement. I was bored, nervous and sort of felt like I was dreaming. The police station made me feel like I was in the midst of a thriller or a mystery. I kept expecting to see clues from homicide cases pinned up on the walls. There were mostly just calendars and flyers for training exercises in the office I was held up in till 2 AM. Finally, Jessica arrived to take me to my next home.

I ended up back in South Central Los Angeles, about three blocks away from where my grandma was taking care of her mother, in my great grandmother's house. Right from the start, I felt uncomfortable at my new home. A single woman named Ethel lived there with her twenty-year-old son named Jamar. Ethel was heavy-set, kind of tall, and seemed mostly depressed. She had a raspy voice and was grumpy much of the time. Over the three months that I was there I developed headaches from her indoor chain smoking. The constant fog of gray smoke wrapped itself around me like an inescapable phantom. Everywhere I turned, there it was, gaping at me with toxicity, forcing me into suffocation.

Jamar stayed in his room with the door closed most of the time. I could hear people sneaking in and out of his window day and night. It sounded like they were partying and acting immature. It was wintertime and I was out of school because of my new school trimester schedule. On the weekends, Ethel's nephew, DeShawn, would come stay and sleep in the same room as me on another bed. DeShawn was about eight or nine and had already begun his decline into kleptomania and sleight of hand. After one weekend I noticed that my shoes were missing. After another weekend, my jacket was missing. Finally he swiped a hidden cellphone I had for calling my siblings, grandmother, Danger and Kate. This was when I lost it.

"Did you take my cellphone, DeShawn?" I asked him in the living room where he was playing video games. Jamar came out of his room when he heard my voice call out in anger. They'd never witnessed much of my emotional spectrum. I mostly kept to myself and stayed quiet.

"No, man," DeShawn said without taking his eyes off the TV. "Don't know what the heck you're talking about, man."

This infuriated me. "DeShawn, I know you took my shoes, my jacket, and my cellphone and I want them back right now bro."

Jamar piped in, "Marquis, you should kick DeShawn's ass for taking your shit."

I looked at him with a confused look on my face. What was he trying to accomplish?

"Come on, man," Jamar continued to egg me on. "You gonna take this stuff from a punk ass kid? Teach him a lesson."

A few of Jamar's friends piled out of the small room and started punching their fists into their palms. "Yeah," they echoed, "kick his ass, Marquis."

I wasn't sure what was happening, and then some of Jamar's friends picked up DeShawn and started pumping him up with fighting words. "You going to take some foster kid's accusations?" they asked. "You better show Marquis who is boss, man."

I felt a stirring in my chest and before I knew it DeShawn lunged on top of me and started punching me. I wrestled him around until I was sitting on his chest, wailing on his face and yelling that I wanted my things back now. The twenty-year-old boys gathered around the fight, yelping and whooping. They'd gotten exactly what they were after: two young boys beating the heck out of each other.

By the time we were both red and bruised I'd had enough. Part of me wanted to beat up Jamar and his friends, but I knew they were too big for me. The other part of me wanted to cry. I decided to get the hell out of there and run to my great grandmother's house to be with Cleo. I made my escape and lunged out the front door at lightning speeds. My feet dashed the three blocks away with perfect precision and ease. It was easy to run away from that which was so blatantly wrong and messed up. By the time I rushed into Cleo's arms I was a blubbering mess.

My grandmother hugged me hard and said she'd call Jessica. To my surprise the social worker said I could stay with Cleo until she found a new place for me. I was so happy and excited I almost didn't know what to do with myself. The relief of being in a safe place changed my physiology. My headaches went away, my heart rate decreased and I didn't feel like I was always on the lookout for possible attacks. Being in those foster homes for the most part was like being a domesticated caged animal living in the wild. I was always on guard, always looking around me, wandering what type of predator lay waiting in the brush. My cortisol levels were constantly through the roof. I was in fight-or-flight mode seventy-five percent of the time. I'd forgotten what it was like to feel secure and protected. I'd forgotten what it felt like to know what home really was.

CHAPTER 6

"Being humbled has been a part of my life for a long time."

– Lamar Odom

My time with Cleo was short lived. Within forty-eight hours Jessica came to pick me up. I dropped to my knees onto the floor and let the river of suppressed emotions flow. I couldn't do it. I couldn't go back out there again. This was my home, why did they want to keep taking me away from the nest? I cried and cried and my body shook as Cleo and Jessica both choked up at my sorrow. This was the first time I had witnessed a social worker display this type of emotion. They both took my arms and gave me hugs, but they both agreed that for the time being, I needed to go.

I sat in Jessica's car while she went back in to talk to Cleo privately. Jessica asked Cleo if there was anything she could do to get Danger and I back. Through tears she told my grandmother that it would be better for everyone if we were able to move back home. Cleo said she would try her hardest to find another place to live that would accommodate us boys. When Jessica returned to the car she told me what Cleo had said. It made me feel hopeful. I decided that if I could tough it out for a little longer, I'd be back home in no time.

Jessica dropped me off at a group home in Chino Hills, California. I was there for about five or six months. During this time Cleo went back to court with Jessica, who made recommendations to the judge, insisting that reuniting would be best for everyone. Cleo was working with an organization that paid her for in-house elderly care, which was how she was making money while living with her disabled mother. My great grandmother's home was too small for all of us though, so Cleo worked hard to find a place for us to live.

The group home was not considered a foster home, but a temporary place for foster kids to stay. There were eight other kids at the home and there was a small staff, each of which worked different shifts. The manager took us to school in the mornings and when we got back to the home there were supervisors there until 10 or 11 PM when the night staff arrived. These were not individuals with specific certifications or license; they were just a group of staff that genuinely cared about giving back and helping youth.

I began my time there at the end of the 6th grade and into summer school. Surprisingly, I liked it there. It was well structured and the other kids were just like me for the most part. They were all in the same boat at least. We weren't bound to one parent or family, we didn't have to compete for attention, biological children weren't picked over us —we simply were wards of the court, whether temporary or permanently.

In this specific boy's home I was the youngest, aged twelve. The teenagers were fifteen to sixteen years old on average. At first there was a little contention, teasing and bullying, because I was little and thin. The older boys would challenge me by asking if I was in a gang or about my extracurricular activities. I did what I always did, stayed quiet and stuck to myself. After a couple weeks we were all getting along just fine.

The way the home worked was very organized and everyone knew what was expected of him. We had whiteboards with schedules, chores, and meals written on them. We were motivated by a goal system. If we did all of our chores; got up on time, completed homework assignments, and were generally amiable, we'd get points. At the end of the week we'd go on outings and play sports, go to museums or amusement parks, and our points would be converted into money. This was a pretty efficient reward system, and there was a common collective feeling of support that challenged and inspired each of us. We were also treated equally. To the employees and staff, we were their responsibility, and they were being watched and monitored to make sure they did their jobs right. The system worked because it was team-oriented.

I made friends with my roommate who was a few years older than me. We'd stay up talking about sports and music. There was a basketball court outside the home so all the guys would shoot hoops together in the afternoon and evenings. Once again, I was changing. I felt hopeful and there was a seed of purpose growing inside of me. I intrinsically knew that the foster care system was set up strangely and that it had brought more distress than comfort to me. These epiphanies were only glimmers floating through my consciousness, but the seed had been planted, and my experiences at the boy's home had provided sunlight, water, and nourishment.

A brotherly camaraderie naturally developed between myself and the eight other teenagers. It was like we'd all survived the apocalypse where our families had disappeared. Now we were forming bonds with each other, finding inspiration in each other, and creating familial relationships not based on exclusion or elitism. We were a global family, a team of teenagers functioning and thriving in a professional environment that wouldn't permit abuse or any questionable parenting styles. It worked. It worked because it was out in the open, and because it was honest.

Finally after almost a year Cleo found a place for us all to live. Jessica picked me up and took me to my new home in south central Los Angeles. Driving down the highway I felt my heart swell. Was it really over? Had it been a dream? A nightmare? Or perhaps it'd been something in between? I felt like Frodo, soaring in the gentle clutches of a giant eagle. I was being pulled back home to the Shire where normality would ensue. How could one think of things like college, career, or the future when their immediate environment is consumed with constant struggle? Looking back now, I realize that I had no conception of a long-term future; I was only capable of digesting what was occurring moment to moment.

Jessica sat in the driver's seat quietly, taking in her victory. She was like a hero in many ways. The wise social worker knew what was right, and she'd stood her ground and wielded her staff to help me arrive back home. There was a look of peace and serenity in her dark brown eyes. In her mind she was probably thinking, "Yes, I've saved another one." She was right.

The apartment complex in South Central LA was new and very nice. Jessica guided me through the buildings until we arrived at Cleo's front door. As soon as it swung open I saw Danger on the other side. I dropped my things and hugged him as hard as I could. We were so happy to be back. Cleo showed us the apartment and led us into our own rooms. It was the first time I'd had my own room in quite a while. Jessica said her goodbyes and the little family was alone. We couldn't stop smiling. Each one of us was beaming. It almost felt like it was too good to be true. But it wasn't, it was real.

That night Cleo took Danger and me out to Hometown Buffet to celebrate. I loaded up on fried chicken, pizza, and spaghetti and meatballs. I filled my belly as if I were filling my soul with joy and faith. When I was at the foster homes I didn't have much of an appetite, but being back with my loved ones made it very easy to once again enjoy the fruits of life. For dessert I filled bowl after bowl with vanilla ice cream, Oreo crumbs, and bits of almonds. It was delicious. We feasted, laughed, and relished in the light of a warm hearth, the love that connected us.

From here things changed completely. I felt great physically and it seemed that the story of my young life had concluded into a happy ending. I started the 7th grade at a new school and started to do better academically. I bonded with Danger and after a while it was like nothing had ever changed between us. Cleo seemed softer in many ways, as if she too had endured the trials and conflicts of an epoch as well.

I was filled with optimism; so much so that I did what most people do when they're out of a traumatic or crisis situation. I forgot. I blocked out the past from my mind and made myself not think about it. I was still too young to really digest how those years had altered me. Most nights in the foster homes I cried when I went to bed. I didn't want to think about that. I was home now, and I had positive things to look forward to.

Socially I was struggling at school. I felt disconnected from the others because there weren't really any transplants, they were mostly kids who'd all grown up together. I felt estranged, partly because of my innate shyness, but also because of the foster care system experiences. I was at a fragile age where adolescence was blossoming and gangs and cliques were strong. During lunch I'd sit in a classroom by myself in order to avoid social interaction. I think part of the trauma that developed from moving so much and living with people I didn't know was that I developed a fear of strangers and new people. It was very hard to get close to anyone I didn't know.

Danger acclimated much better to the social world than I did. At this time Danger was nine and was placed on the honor roll at his elementary school. He was very active and outgoing. He was always hanging out with friends and having fun outside. I spent most of my time indoors watching TV. I don't remember feeling depressed; I just preferred my own company. It is possible that Danger received more nurturing while in the foster system because he was so little and dependent. Danger claimed that he had fun in the homes and that the experience wasn't bad, so I trusted him.

My biological mother, Sherry, came back into our lives. She'd visit a few times a year. The interactions were much better, this was primarily due to the fact that she'd been clean and sober for a while. Sherry had healthy interactions and conversations with us; she was no longer erratic or violent. Sherry and Cleo got along for the most part, but every now and then they'd have a fight and a falling out. Always though, they'd eventually patch things up. Sherry had finally come to understand that financially and legally, she couldn't take care of Danger and me, and also that we preferred to live with our grandmother.

Kate had moved back to Los Angeles, and we continued to stay in touch. Shortly after due to a misunderstanding between Cleo and her, I didn't see her for a year. That summer a man in our apartment complex asked me if I wanted to make some extra money. He said he ran a non-profit organization for children and that he needed us kids (the others in the complex) to sell candy for donations. We'd make a percentage and he'd pocket the rest. He would round us up after school and drive us to wealthy parts of town like Santa Monica to take advantage of the rich. One day I ran into one of Kate's friends, also a teacher from the elementary school I went to. The teacher told Kate, and then Kate called Cleo to tell her that it wasn't good for me to be involved in this man's schemes.

Kate told Cleo that I could come work for her at the school where she was working as the principal, and that this would be a much better alternative to selling candy. Cleo misinterpreted Kate's intentions and thought Kate was threatening to call social services. Cleo thought a social worker was getting involved and that Kate was trying to cause problems. This wasn't the case, but Cleo was very sensitive about this and she told me not to speak to Kate because of it. I didn't understand what was going on, but eventually it blew over and we began to spend weekends with Kate again.

Between the age of thirteen and fifteen, not a lot happened. I still didn't have many friends and I was attending a huge school, which actually made it harder to get to know anyone. At this point I was definitely experiencing social anxiety. I felt nervous at school all the time and went to great lengths to avoid crowds. I spent a lot of time on the school computer playing games like solitaire or pinball. My love for basketball didn't go away though, and I'd play a few games at school. While on the court I didn't think about my place socially, I only thought of the hoop and the ball. I signed up to be on a three-month park league team for a while too, although I didn't bond with anyone enough to hang out outside of the games.

My grandmother still went to church faithfully, but Danger and I opted to sleep in on

Sundays. I wasn't focused at the time on my religion or any kind of divine being; I was just trying to survive life day to day. Basketball was at the center of my daily routine and after some research I decided to attend the first ever Kobe Bryant Camp in L.A. I was still selling candy and I'd saved up a little bit of money. The camp would last two weeks and cost $400. I signed up and filled out the application. I paid the fee and after a week or two I received an email saying I'd been accepted.

A weekend in Venice, California (2004)

CHAPTER 7

———

"The most important thing is to try and inspire people so that they can be great in whatever they want to do."

-Kobe Bryant

K obe Bryant was my hero. For as long as I could remember he'd been my favorite player on my favorite team: The Los Angeles Lakers. I was ecstatic at the possibility of meeting him, but overall I was thrilled to be attending such an awesome camp. I was fifteen and on the verge of adulthood. I was introverted and quiet, but also passionate and naturally empathetic. For most of my life I'd been around female caretakers, but I had never really had a strong consistent male role model. Even though

I'd never met him, Kobe Bryant was the closest thing to what I'd aspire to be when I was a young teenager. It wasn't that I wanted to be a famous basketball player; I wasn't sure what I wanted to do yet. It was that as far as respected, insightful men went, Kobe was the best. He had an air about him, and he aimed for benevolence. The camp really was an expression of his best attributes.

The camp was stationed on the campus of Loyola Marymount University during the summer of 2007. I recall hitching a ride from a neighbor and being dropped off in front of the campus. I felt sweaty and nervous, but also excited. I really didn't know what to expect. Aside from the fact that I was going to be surrounded by hundreds of strangers, it was actually the first camp I'd ever been a part of. It was a treat, something I was giving myself, and that in itself felt odd.

I followed the other pre-teens and teenagers with their backpacks and basketballs towards the check-in area. After standing in line and showing our printed off stubs to verify identification, we all headed to the gymnasium. We sat waiting for about an hour. Most of the boys were sitting quietly on the bleachers, staring straight ahead. There was a kind of reverence permeating the gym, and great admiration for what was to come. It became apparent at that point that national or international, each one of us was a major basketball enthusiast.

Eventually, Kobe Bryant walked in wearing a yellow and purple jersey with his famous lucky number 24 printed on his abdomen. Everyone went wild, stood and applauded him. Kobe stood six-foot, six-inches tall and had a grin plastered across his docile face. With microphone in hand he did what he did best and riled up the crowd. "Whaddup, whaddup, whaddup? How ya'all doin'? You guys ready for a great summer or what?"

The young men around me shot up out of their seats whooping, and yelled back, "YEAH!"

"Alright!" He said, "Now just so you all know, I'm here to answer any questions you might have. You ask anything, I'll give you an answer. Let's get settled in and we'll talk about the schedule."

We returned to our seats and from there Kobe turned the microphone over to a coach to go over rules and what we'd be doing over the next few days. Next we were split into three different league groups based on our age. There were about 500 boys and girls there, aged eight to eighteen. After the greeting we were led to our dorm rooms where we'd be rooming with three others. I set down my things and rested for a minute before we were to head down for lunch. Over the next few days, our schedule went as follows: up at 7 AM, breakfast in the cafeteria, meet in the gym to go over the schedule and do stretches, break into groups and teams and practice drills and plays, eat lunch, participate in a game with another team, and then in the evening we'd witness a speech or indulge in some kind of entertainment like watching a basketball movie. That first night, Kobe played a pick-up game with other famous basketball players like Luke Walton, Mark Jackson, Trevor Ariza and Kobe's dad.

After a few days I befriended another teenager my age from China. His name was Ling and he spoke English well. I had not had much experience in meeting people from around the world, but the camp offered this to me. I learned a lot about different cultures and how people interacted differently. Ling and I became buddies with a few others, but mostly, everyone got along. Everyone that attended was a huge Lakers or

Kobe fan, so we all had something in common. We were shown how to work together as a team and how to watch each other's backs. This was right after Hurricane Katrina happened, so Kobe had even flown out a group of kids who'd been affected for free. All of the young men were just elated to be there.

The speeches were given by other basketball players or coaches, and were mostly aimed at encouraging us to stay focused, develop our skills and to stay on the right path. They emphasized the importance of staying away from drugs and alcohol, as well as gangs. Kobe Bryant's high school basketball coach, Gregg Downer, especially impressed me. Just the fact that Kobe's own high school coach had stuck with him for so long, and inspired him when he was just a kid was mindboggling. Gregg was very inspiring and had a great sense of humor. He believed that there were philosophies in basketball that mirrored the philosophies of life. His belief in Kobe and the importance of teamwork was what really struck me.

About halfway through the camp, I had a moment with Kobe. Mr. Bryant was watching a game I was playing in. It was towards the end of the game and my team was doing well. I could feel Kobe watching me, so I tried to impress him by doing my signature crossover dribbling and shooting a fade-away jump shot. I was feeling pretty cool.

After the game Kobe gave me a high-five and said, "I saw you make that shot. Nice job, man!"

The moment was a bit surreal, but I took the opportunity to talk to him more. I said, "Thank you. Hey Kobe, you think the U.S. team will win at the Olympics next year?"

Kobe grinned and said, "We better win. I'm very competitive."

I nodded and dug into another area that I was dying to know. "If you leave the Lakers, will you continue this camp next year?"

There was a sparkle in his eyes as he told me, "Oh yeah, this is going to be an every year thing. So you make sure to come back next year, alright?"

I said, "Yup," just as a group of other campers came rushing over to talk to Kobe. Just a few weeks prior to the camp Kobe had announced in a radio interview that he wanted to be traded to a different team. I wanted to ask him more questions but the other campers were tugging on him. Eventually, someone with a camera started taking pictures. I got one with just Kobe and me. I was floating. It was one of the greatest moments of my young life.

At the end of the camp we were each given feedback about our basketball skills and team contribution. The coaches told me that I brought a lot of energy and positivity to the team, and that I should keep up the good work. They also told me I needed to work on my dribbling skills. I took the information and channeled it into self-improvement, although by this point I was already feeling pretty awesome. The camp had been life changing for me. It helped me build character and to become more social. I connected with the group and was forced to interact. It was easy though, because we were all brought to the same point at the same time with the same passion and understanding: sure basketball is just a game, but in many ways, so is life. We were learning how to be smart, think on our toes, work together, and make the shot. I returned from that camp a different kid, because intrinsically—I had learned how to believe in myself.

From this point on I felt motivated to do better at everything. I returned to the Kobe Bryant Basketball Camp for two years after that, until I graduated high school. Each year, I learned more about myself, the challenges of life, and most importantly, how to function in a team. I feel now that the camp was actually the impetus for wanting to go to college. Kate was always encouraging higher education as well, and it was these two motivating and inspiring entities that ushered me towards academic ascension. The idea of going to college before this just seemed extremely far-fetched. I couldn't see myself in that way. I had never thought of myself as smart or brainy. Plus in the areas I grew up, a very small percentage of high school students went on to pursue degrees beyond a GED or high school diploma.

My sophomore year in high school, I attended Locke High School in South Central L.A with 3,000 kids in it. The conditions were horrible. The school was failing and there weren't even enough seats for students to sit on during class. It was overloaded and poorly run. Eventually it was taken over by a charter organization. If you weren't on track with their requirements (A, B-average) you were asked to find a different school to attend. Luckily there was a new public charter school with the L.A Alliance network that opened up just down the street from my house. I signed up and got in at the start of my junior year in 2008.

This school was much smaller, only about 400 students. It was a high school, but it was also called a college prep school, or a college-ready academy. The bar was raised and I was given a lot of attention on how to bring up my GPA and prepare for college. In this school, a C- or below was considered a fail, so we all spent a lot of time doing our best work. Because it was small, the teachers had ample time to encourage and tutor the students. For the first time I felt like I was actually pretty intelligent, and that a lot of people were rooting for me. My social anxiety was practically nonexistent, and I was feeling so much better about everything. I made friends and enjoyed camaraderie and getting to know new people. I even played on the basketball team my junior and senior years.

Pictured with Kobe Bryant in 2007, at his first-ever youth basketball camp

Vanessa Bryant and me (L-R)

CHAPTER 8

"Every time you compete, try harder to improve on your last performance. Give nothing short of your very best effort "

- Elgin Baylor

A s the end of my senior year drew closer, administrators and counselors helped me prepare for college. Even after doing really well the last few years, my GPA was still 1.9. Odds were slim that I'd be accepted anywhere other than community college. I decided to do my own research and found a program within the California State University system called the Educational Opportunity Program. Only a few campuses had special admission consideration for students with unique life circumstances, so I applied within this program to Cal State Northridge. The application process was very lengthy. I had to complete multiple questionnaires and an in-person interview. Initially, I was nervous about applying since there were only 160 spots available and thousands of applicants. After receiving multiple denial letters from all other universities, this was my last hope. Exactly one month before my high school graduation I received a letter in the mail stating I had been accepted into the EOP program and the University on the condition of successfully completing the summer phase program.

The six-week summer program was life changing for me to say the least. I lived on campus, took college courses, met great peers and was provided student mentors who also shared similar backgrounds and life obstacles. In a sense, it felt a lot like my basketball camp experience a few years prior but on a much deeper level. The program not only focused on academics, but also worked with us socially by establishing a supportive community of peers, and instilling values such as Respect, Responsibility, Attitude, and Maturity. These principles would continue to guide me in my first year and the next three years as I steered the complexity of being a first generation college student.

In addition to the EOP Program, I was also accepted into the Resilient Scholars Program. The Resilient Scholars Program specifically helps former foster youth by providing an additional layer of support services for students and links to campus resources. "Without support services, less than 5% of all foster youth who attend a four-year university go on to graduate from college." I refused to be a part of the 95%. This program at the time was in its early stages of being established on campus but nonetheless, the commitment and dedication demonstrated by the staff towards helping us succeed was one of the most inspiring experiences. It felt great being in a space where I was genuinely able to put my guard down and really connect with other people. Engaging with other students who also grew up in foster care felt powerful. We were driven to change the statistics about us – we were all determined to graduate from the university.

We had weekly meetings together and it felt as though we were occupying a world of our own. We spoke, told stories, shared our challenges and helped one another get through tough times. We also studied, volunteered, and worked on several projects for the advancement of the community. Because we had gone through relatable experiences, being together made us feel more motivated to succeed. One of the things this involvement on campus taught me is that having people around for support is invaluable and it is sometimes all that is needed to have a different outcome. We were truly the definition of resilient.

During my freshman year, I was often worried about not passing a class or failing a test. Eventually, these fears subsided as I became more confident in my abilities. I received a lot of support and encouragement from mentors and friends. My past really felt distant at this point and I really believed that I could accomplish whatever I set out to do. With focus and determination to succeed, I finished my first semester as a freshman with a 4.0 GPA. For the first time in a while, I felt like a true champion. But I knew this was only the beginning. I continued to flourish during my time in college and became heavily involved on and off campus by mentoring others and even going back to my community to speak and advocate on behalf of higher education.

In 2014, I graduated in 4 years with a bachelor's degree in Recreation & Tourism Management with a 3.4 GPA. After college, I went on to work in different capacities, supporting and helping youth. I was the first of my 5 siblings to graduate from a 4-year university and only one of my other siblings has graduated from high school.

As I grew into adulthood, I became closer to Kate, who became a best friend and a mother. She officially adopted me in the summer of 2012, when I was twenty and we currently remain in close contact. Cleo continues to be a proud grandmother and is more supportive than ever before. Sherry has been clean for many years now and we have a great relationship as well. Once I left the house and went to college, Danger dropped out of school and began to get into trouble. Sometimes I felt guilty for leaving the home to attend school because I was like a positive role model to him, and without the added motivation, Danger began to change. I think it is possible that since he was so much younger in the foster care system, and he'd been taken away from his support system so early, it made him reliant on others. He hadn't developed in a conventional way—of course, I hadn't either.

It took me a long time to tell the people closest to me that I had forgiven them; I love them or even open up to share my true emotions. For years I would avoid uttering those three words. Now as an adult, I see the importance of verbalizing your affections and letting the people you love know that you care about them. I have learned so much from my experiences in life, and as a young adult, I see myself taking the wisdom that I've gained and doing everything I can to bring about change for the children of this world. I feel that there is a lot more work to be done to bring about change in the foster care system. In some cases, the needs of children in foster care placements are overlooked and I believe that more focus needs to be placed on it. However, it starts with advocacy and reform.

The end of High School (2010)
– Heritage College Ready Academy

(2013) California State University Northridge

95

CHAPTER 9

———

"I've seen a lot in my life. I've seen a lot of winning.
I've seen a lot of testing times. I think when you're
tested, you really find out what you're made of. "

– Jerry West

A 2010 study conducted in the states of Iowa, Wisconsin, and Illinois followed 600 young adults who had aged out of the child welfare system. The statistics from the study showed that after the age of twenty-three or twenty-four, less than half were employed, nearly twenty-five percent were homeless, more than seventy-five percent of women had gotten pregnant since leaving foster care, nearly sixty percent of men were convicted of a crime, and more than eighty percent had been arrested.

Also, only six percent had a two or four-year degree. Emancipated foster youth were also found to have a ten percent higher rate of using illegal drugs than the national average.

The above results reflect one fact; the system is not working. A system that churns out more than fifty percent of negative outcomes is not worthy to be commended. There are not enough discussions about the repercussions and statistics of men and women who were once in foster care. If as a community we want to lessen crime, substance abuse, unplanned pregnancies, and increase education, then we need to start with the foster care system. The displacement of a child in many cases from a sense of belonging is creating dislocated individuals. We need to create a loving environment for youth to find a connection. Healing needs to be key as well as consistent bonds . In foster homes, the problems of the past are rarely addressed and primarily swept under the rug because it's easier that way. Foster youth should be encouraged to think about the future, to harness their innate talents and intelligence, and to consider what they want to do with their lives. Support and assistance will ultimately change the way they think.

These suggestions are not just for the children; they're for this country, and for the world at large. If we want improved individuals, it has to start with our most vulnerable youth population. We have to give those who come from difficult environments the opportunity to overcome what was out of their hands to begin with. We have to see these children as our communal responsibility, to bring them to a state of wellness in the aftermath of a disaster. Another study shows that seventy-five percent of Connecticut youths in criminal justice systems were once in the foster care system. Illinois found that eighty percent of juvenile prisoners had spent time in foster care. It is evident changes need to be made. The next four recommendations will highlight ways of making the foster care system more approachable, and positive in general.

1) Rebrand the Present-Day Foster Care System by Creating a New "Face"

One of the biggest challenges of today's foster care is the fact that the system does not have a positive image. There's no known face or public figure aggressively fighting for its causes or issues. There are tons of celebrities and politicians publicly advocating for issues like children's hospitals and many other important topics that affect the society. Though these efforts are commendable and very much needed, they currently have a great deal of awareness and backing, which has ultimately rallied the public to take some form of action. Even though there are countless successful non-profit organizations whose missions and work make a difference every day, the concern is that the majority of the general public is not aware of the devastating statistics facing foster youth, particularly on a national level. This is why the idea of rebranding and using a positive face to represent the system could encourage a lot of suitable parents and supporters who might have previously been reluctant to get involved, to become engaged, thereby offering the much-needed support to our youth.

2) Support for Foster Care Parents & Social Workers

Being a foster parent or parent, in general, is not easy. Having a child thrown into your life is transformative, but can also cause breakdown or burnout if you're not properly prepared. There needs to a better support system in place.

Unfortunately, such support is not always available and in some states, it's even hard to come by for social workers that struggle with massive caseloads. An alternative option to the current one in place would be to have a consistent part-time family on call who have gone through the appropriate screening process and can take on children for a night or weekend to regularly give foster parents breaks when needed. Traditional family units have this option through relatives or friends. Currently, if caretakers need to have temporary personal time away, children are relocated to what is called respite care, which serves as a temporary housing. However, providing a second family for additional support and advice ultimately benefits all parties involved.

3) Improve the Regulations and Procedures of Placements to Mirror Traditional Families.

There are so many policies, procedures, rules, and regulations for placements and foster youth often feel they don't have control over their own lives. Lawyers, social workers, psychiatrists, guardians, doctors, foster parents and judges all have a say on what is best for them. Paperwork and approval is required for the simplest things, such as playing on a sport's team or obtaining a driver's license. This takes away from the normality a child craves, it makes him or her feel unusual, and also creates confusion. If a foster child or teenager wants to have a say in his or her own choices, it can be very difficult. We need to find a way to cut back on the number of people who control these youths lives and give more responsibility to fewer individuals.

4) Family Reunification

When a child is moved from his or her biological family unit, it can be devastating. Typically, this movement is due to parents going to jail, abusing drugs, or being abusive or neglectful. The weight of enduring this type of trauma is hard enough on a child or teen, but for them to be told directly or indirectly that they can no longer reside with their family is also tough. We need to focus on the hope and probability that reunification with their biological family is possible once their home is safe. Oftentimes people refer to aging out and adoption as the goal, and they overlook reunification with their biological parent or a relative. Half of all foster care children are eventually reunited with their biological families.

In my personal experience, reunification with a family member was considered the last option but in reality, this changed the course of my path for the better. So the conversation needs to be different.

Just as there is no particular right way to be a good parent, there is also no simple recipe for how to fix the system. Every child is different and each situation is unique and should be approached on an individualized basis. That said, there are qualities, or ingredients parents should possess when caring for a child. Reflecting back on my time in foster care, if there were five traits I could recommend to my former caregivers, it would be the following below. While these might seem like common sense, reflecting and improving these qualities within trainings or workshops is important, especially for the benefit of foster youth's.

Perseverance

When a kid walks through a foster home for the first time, they are entering a strange environment after leaving a potentially scary one. It is up to the caretaker not to give up or quickly resort to removal from the home as the only solution despite the emotional hardships.

Patience

As the old saying goes, patience is a virtue. Patience has to extend to their emotional well-being as well. Many of the youth in foster care have suffered emotional or physical abuses the likes of which some of us cannot imagine. That makes it all the more important to remain patient while working with this population.

Understanding

Empathy and understanding with anyone will go a long way in creating a healthy and happy environment. Understanding one's needs is paramount to being able to show them you care.

Communication

Communication is key in any healthy relationship. It's also important for a caretaker to be unafraid to ask questions and know that resources are available when needed. No parent should raise a child alone, and foster parents are no exception.

Love

Without love, the above four qualities are unconnected. With love, these qualities come naturally. It's love that helps parents persevere through those difficult times and find the patience and understanding to communicate with their child. It's through love that trust is built and lives are changed for the better.

It is my hope that through education, advocacy, and awareness, we can awaken the world to the issues and dilemmas in the foster care system. If you are able, become involved, spread the word, and inform others. If you grew up in the foster care system, know that it might have in no way been perfect, but there is no shame in seeking out the available resources so that you can find fulfillment. If you are a foster parent, know that we appreciate what you do, and we understand that the journey is not easy. Finally, if you are a social worker, work with your fellow professionals in finding ways to care for yourselves, particularly in this field of work because it is very common to feel burnout and it takes courage to take on a career so emotionally draining. It is important to continue to push forward with a purpose in mind so that you can perform your best for your clients. To the rest of the world, go out of your way to find out how to connect with local organizations and agencies that support foster youth. Friendship and healthy relationships is key to overcoming hardship or trauma of any kind. Let's go out and make these changes together.

EOP Resilient Scholar and Academic Mentor, Marquis Williams featured as a CSUN Outstanding Grad

May 14, 2014

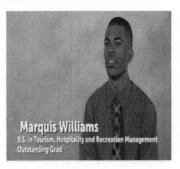

Marquis Williams
B.S. in Tourism, Hospitality and Recreation Management
Outstanding Grad

Read the write-up on Marquis' accomplishments on CSUN Today's website: http://csunshinetoday.csun.edu/media-releases/hard-work-and-determination-pays-off-for-csuns-newest-graduates/

Kate, Me, Cleo and Sherry (L-R) at my college graduation.

Me, Cleo and Danger (L-R) (2015)

Made in the USA
San Bernardino, CA
02 July 2020